Plumb Level and Square

Trent Busch

Cyberwit.net
HIG 45 Kaushambi Kunj, Kalindipuram
Allahabad - 211011 (U.P.) India
http://www.cyberwit.net
Tel: +(91) 9415091004 +(91) (532) 2552257
E-mail: info@cyberwit.net

Printed at Repro India Limited.

Again, to Carol

AUTHOR'S NOTE

Most of my friends live in my shop: the table saw, joiner, lathe, router, chisels, even that whimsical shop vac that is the subject of one of the poems in this book. They don't often talk back, except when it's my fault. However dangerous they are, they are my friends and have some remarkable secrets and unusual points of view. They seem to know that I rid myself of many problems by using them in my woodworking and seem to realize that I love them as well as the wood I work with. This mutual understanding ties in with the poems that come out of that union. It's almost as if each tool has a story too.

I have many types of poems, of course; I don't write exclusively about the tools in my workshop. I was not born a woodworker, and there are none in my family. Similarly, instead of writing classes, I've followed Howard Nemerov's advice when he told me to "read long and then deep maybe." Working with wood and tying that joy into my poetry somehow became an avenue for writing more poems.

Just let me say that I love making poems in the same way that I love building things from wood, as I loved the baby bed, the high chair, the rocking horse, the full size bed, and the cedar chest that I made for my granddaughter as she grew up. The poetry and tools offer me finished products that make up the menagerie that supplies me with a world of friends.

Trent Busch

Others I wish to thank for these pages: Orton Jones, Mick Loggins, Clint Nicely, Laura Carper, Bret Busch, James Carper, Peyton Carper, Jody Fausett, Faye Echols, Peter and Melissa Epes, Bill Fuller, Gerry Webb, Rodney, Kendall, and Judie, Larry Lemasters, Rob Maxwell, Jorena Simpkins, Kelli White, and Dr. Karunesh Kumar Agarwal.

Thanks to the editors of the following publications where poems, sometimes with different titles and in different form, first appeared:

American Journal of Nursing: "Clarence II"
The American Scholar: "I.T. Davis"
The Bellingham Review, "The Death of the Wood Rasp"
Birmingham Poetry Review: "Dust"
The Boston Review: "Bookcase"
Bryant Literary Review: "House on Munday Road"
Crab Creek Review: "Splinter in the Hand"
Dash Literary Journal: "A Piece of Cherry"
Engaging Poetry: "I.T. Davis"
Grist Journal: "The Cardinal"
The Grove Review: "What Used to Be There"
Gulf Coast: "Plumb Level and Square"
Hawai'i Review: "The Whittler"
Hole in the Head Review, "Visitor"
indicia: "Tomorrow, A Sofa Table"
Isthmus: "Season's Colors"
Kansas Quarterly: "A Late Morning Neighbor"
The Kennesaw Review: "Clarence"
Kindred Magazine: "Snake"
Los Angeles Review: "Cut Once"
Margaret Reid First Place Poetry Prize: "Edges of Roads"
The Massachusetts Review: "Le Breun Speaks of King Tut"
Midway Journal: "Le Breun Talks to Himself"
Midwest Quarterly: "The Box"
Minnetonka Review: "Mr. Cooper" and "Gluing"
Missing Spoke: "Uncle Arthur"

Mount Hope Review: "The Whittler" and "Shop Vac"

Nine Cloud Journal: *"Workplace"*

Nomans Journal: "What the Board Does"

North American Review: "The Sighter from Munday"

The Northwest Review: "Summer Storm"

Notre Dame Review: "Mutiny" and "Rocking Horse"

Pinyon: "Fossil in Cement"

Poetry: "Woman in a Swing"

Poetry Daily: "Bookcase"

Prairie Schooner: "The Hound at the Gate"

The Raven's Perch: "Flipping the Switch" and "Shop Window"

Red Wheelbarrow: "Sun on the Saw Table"

San Pedro River Review: "Kick Back"

Santa Fe Literary Review: Ed from the Garage Comes by to Talk Philosophy"

Slant: "Grandfather Ghost"

Shenandoah, "Workshop"

Snake Nation Review: "Edges of Roads"

Soundings Review: "Natural"

Southern Humanities Review: "The Break"

The Southern Review, "Howard Nemerov"

The Sow's Ear Poetry Review: "And So Good-Bye . . ."

The Threepenny Review: "The Uncle"

The West Texas Literary Review: "Chest of Drawers"

Under a Warm Green Linden: "Grindstone"

Winning Writers: "Edges of Roads"

Wraparound South: "Smell"

IN MEMORY OF HOWARD NEMEROV

At forty-five, Nemerov,
you were teaching me, though
you won't remember that,
or my name, or that we sat
on a wall at a school
in a western state where
I tried to listen hard.

You have won the prize now
and were pleased, or so your
son said as he spoke on
educational TV,
a show about you as poet
where you walked a lot
and other people talked.

What I want to say (I
feel like a fool calling
you Sir), Nemerov, is
I am glad for you, though
you were never kind to
me, or unkind, as I
am glad for anyone

who is rewarded when
he is worthy, the mower
whose scythe hugs the ground, the
engineer whose bridge does
not, after twenty years,

collapse with a hundred
cars into the river.

Now I am forty-five.
Perhaps I didn't listen
hard enough, your advice
about reading long, then
deep, maybe; perhaps no
one can be taught much by
another, but I wish you

to know your sure step there
drew me into the drama:
I like an Elizabethan
player watching that other
actor as he paused, then
turned and disappeared down
some lost street in Stratford.

Contents

1 Aging Boarders

SEASON'S COLORS

On the anvil in the corner
horseshoes were made
and on the homemade saw table
a house was built.

Now not much use to anyone
except for piling scraps
or flattening a piece of tin

for flashing, yet without help
I lugged them here,
green to season's colors.

The smith who drove nails
between his legs, the joiner
who hung a last door
argue in the shadows.

Let them work a while longer,
I would say were air
not scarce and space not
tight with boxes of complaints
from my own aging boarders.

MR. COOPER

One whiff and I am off;
the scent from the oak board
I have ripped takes me
to a man who with
a handsaw built our house,

a man with lean hands, who
when he took a break sat
with legs crossed and smoked, his
head back, the mystery
of planning in his face.

Usually, I wear my mask;
today I forgot, the scent
of a man in wood caught
in a circle of air
blowing through my shop.

A man younger then than
I am now, he died face
down a week after our house
was built on a path
he took each day to milk.

None to see and mask off, I
draw this portrait for myself:
a small man lighting a smoke,
looking off, the stance
of a winter homemade porch.

THE UNCLE

Work is not a comedy,
he said and rode the hay rake
into the fog, a road
we knew in our minds by heart

from traveling it
in the dark; we followed,
hearing hoofs and the ringing
of wheels upon the rocks.

If in that cave there was
any light—it took us years
to learn to laugh, to hold
a girl, to allow mistakes—

it was in the way we
learned to brush off bats, fear
no ghosts, adjust to damp,
be home in being lost.

Even so, he is here yet,
his heel upon the clutch,
releasing into the midday
sun those long rows that

took our sweat, if not our
hearts, and taught us hate
of levity that in that field
of hay was our success.

CLARENCE

Things he thought
never from inspiration:
no gods, no song,
no Shakespeherian rag.

Had an ear to motors,
carburetors and pistons,
big cat engines,
ring gear timing.

How gutting lawn mowers
saved enough to have a
hand-built house, wife
up roof nailing shingles.

Listen: fact: goddamn
banker didn't know
asshole appetite about
a fuel-injected Mercedes.

No tin stories: jack
the frame and wrench nuts,
stecl ball bearings;
cash in hand, car on
the road his shining.

CLARENCE II

They say you have the big
C now, Clarence, you who
amazed us, tearing
down motors, building up
the ruptured parts, talking
and resting, dragging
deep that first-hand smoke.

How you bragged, Clarence, no
motor you couldn't fix,
and we, marveling, staying
half the night to listen
to it all, jacking you up,
telling everyone we knew.

They say you can't fix this
one, Clarence; they say
you are on your back in
another room where bearings
come only as shipments
in a dream, where now it
is you who must listen.

Christ, Clarence, hell, tell
us what throttles to pull;
how to trick the hoists to
lift, how to free the bolts;
don't lie there choking us
down, you who taught us no
engine was past repair.

They say you won't heed
reason, bruising knuckles,
accelerating, asking for
a thicker manual while
weeds block the windows of
your shop, enshrining your
smoke, remaining the one
place we once wanted to go.

ED FROM THE GARAGE STOPS BY TO TALK PHILOSOPHY

"The tool you order is
never the same in person:
take this wrench here, as
advertised on TV
able to loosen the hind
quarter of a moose, a limp,
pussy-levered fidget
that couldn't jack the nuts
off a sixty-seven Buick;

"just as the person you
get is never the same tool,
whoever he or she
happens to be—I name
no one in particular,
say Lucille Ball, maybe,
or W.H. Auden, huddled
up little round backs with
dip-snuff mouths in a bar."

Now wait a minute, I look
at him, W.H. Auden?

"Hey, man, never think I
don't read my novels;
or that big-boobed Lara
game on the new Playstation:
I'd like to see her climb

up on my roof without
getting anything dirty,
then try to save poor old
Le Breun when he's loaded."

You got me there, I say.

"And a crescent can't be
a monkey wrench like on
that *Parasite Eve*—
but I see I'm losing you here;
the point being, that which
you make must be useful.
Sometimes, friends got to
drop by friends to keep
them on top of reality."

I'm much obliged, I say.

"You don't, it won't set fields
on fire; by example, I'm losing
this wrench faster than a gnat
can lick its ass and remember,
as always, you need me, whistle."

LE BREUN AND THE DELIVERY MAN

Backed up to the door and let off.
I said, What am I supposed
to do with this?
How do I know, the driver said,
all I'm told to do is deliver.
Then, what is it?
Don't know that either,
but I'd get it inside before it rains.
Well, who sent it?
Guy named Smith, that's all I know.
Where'd it come from?
What's all this twenty questions, man,
my foot's in the door, ass's in the seat.
Am I expected to pay for it?
That's your problem,
my guess is by check.
Made out to who?
To whoever. Who you buy it from?
I can't go through that again.
Then sign by the X on the line,
make my job easy one time.
You asked and I'm telling:
that's how I got the goddamn thing.

WHAT USED TO BE THERE

Now, no one lives on the ridges;
houses up the hollow have slumped
into themselves and rabbits feed
above on grass in the cemetery.

After my father's stroke, they put
him in a kind of harness at
the rehabilitation center,
advised a trip out for dinner.

On TV, which he can't follow,
the sit-coms are about families
we don't recognize, unfamiliar
as the reruns of *The Waltons*.

In the rockers on the porch I talk
to him of the willows breaking
into green above the swollen
creeks, redbuds pinking the hardwoods.

I could just as well be talking
about a dried up town where there
was only the taste of salt for
daughters, the saccharine need for

working sons, where wearing a life
was tuneless, decent nights and days
with no thought of memorial.
I could just as well be silent.

BOOKCASE

Dee Dee came by this morning
wanting to know how I
was coming along on her bookcase,
actually not caring, she said,
no hurry, just curious.

Have you ever heard of something
by someone? she asked. You
being a former English teacher
and all, I figured anybody
knew about it, you would.

I hadn't heard of it she was
going to get it anyway,
a reference in there about
a town close to where she grew up
over how many years ago.

That sure was pretty wood that oak,
not like that old pine everybody
told her she could get at Wal-Mart
for half the price, not lasting near
as long, turning out real nice.

Don't let her stop me, she'd be
going, just wanted to stop by
to see if I'd know anything
she ought to buy to put along
side that one we'd talked about,

by the way what was the name
of it again, she couldn't
remember anything these days,
and be sure to inscribe it,
the back maybe, from you to me.

I.T. DAVIS

Since I have time I will
tell you, Grandfather, that
the house is in decay,
road down, saplings trees.

I say since I have time
because over the years
you've kept me so busy
with the occurrences

of hills and woods, I've had
no life to catch you up.
Laura, the two-day-old
you rested on your knees

the night you died, is all
grown up as is her brother
whom you never met but has
your eyes and you would like.

They know some of your days,
but mostly not. Grandfather,
you taught me I must climb
in a world where others sat,

and, climbing, look neither
up nor back, the way maples
keep a close grip on the earth.
If I have done that, I

owe it to your advice,
yet must repeat the sad
news of your house and the road
you so expertly kept,

and remind you too, could
you come back, of a story
you often told about
the lumberjacks that you

marveled at when you were
just a boy, how it was
the ones who held on tight
who were the first to fall.

THE WHITTLER

I always thought you were on verge
of genius, the way you whittled
kittens, sheep, old soldiers to stand
on our window sills as a breeze coaxed
us to dream of storefront Indians.

How could one with such power
on another day pare a pole
down to nothing but shavings, all
the time remaining silent while
loafers on porches ignored you?

Our motive for wishing you full
success was our lack: tops from spools
that wouldn't balance, homemade kites
we wore our soles out raising that,
once flying, remained in branches as
crosspiece decorations for Christmas.

Still I see you, fingering through
small boxes, pausing to drop
a figure in my hand, a dog,
perhaps, stopped in a rainy field
to shake itself, then, catching scent,
running off into mist again.

KICK BACK

The day the triangle of wood
kicked off the saw blade through the screen
into the yard, Uncle Jim had
just turned the corner of the shop.

It wasn't really Uncle Jim,
of course, but you know how there is
always someone in the family
everyone hates to see coming,

usually just after you've bobbed
the tail off the cat or goddamned
some item that was behaving
in a way peculiar to your plan.

You who know can fill in what he
said and how long he took to say
it and what guilt he practically
never left behind when he went on.

Anyway, Uncle Jim was gone
and I was left with a miter
ruined and half a day wasted,
another half needed for the screen,

which I notice this morning I
never got around to, frayed and dusty
so long no one asks about it
now, taking on years and the fate of

the words of Uncle Fake Uncle Jim.
I suppose he exampled us
all once or another, never
guessing the bad we thought he was

doing goodness, cracked in his song,
as if one kick back through a screen
couldn't teach in a second the danger
of a thousand safely cut off ends.

LE BREUN SPEAKS OF KING TUT

I didn't see the King Tut
exhibition but was told
by a student, who usually
in these cases knows more
than the professor, the sight
was plain damn awesome,

and I imagined with the help
of a glance at some show
I have now forgotten
on the Discovery channel
some coffin heavy enough
for a warehouse tractor.

In my ignorance I don't know
what they've done with the body
and should've asked, except
my thoughts were bushwhacked
by that crank Thoreau, you can
look it up, maybe in Emerson,

who, upon the subject of
prolonging your own memory,
was flabbergasted that so many
boobies could degrade themselves
over someone better thrown
in the river or fed to the dogs.

THE SIGHTER FROM MUNDAY

I have been given the job
of Sighter of bees.
It is a job I was
not seeking.

Let me be the man
who saws the tree
when the bees are found,
I said.

Let me be the hive
maker. It was no use
to ask. They had made
other plans.

Every day I go into
the fields and sit by
flowers. I surround
myself with charts,

I make flight plans
and watch the way
bees laden with pollen
bypass the poplars.

I run down hollows
trying to follow,
I search all knotholes
for queens.

The truth is I do not
know what I am doing,
yet every day I
am congratulated:

You are doing a good
job, Henry—which is not
my name—they say. Keep
up the hard work.

I want to say, My name
is not Henry, I want to
tell them, Let me go, bring
back the other Sighter.

But when I speak of him,
I get heavy frowns.
I fear what has happened
to him, what has happened

to me, and I fear even
worse the scar on the heart
of the man they call John,
Inspector of Leaves.

A LATE MORNING NEIGHBOR

Up the bent walk to
the house door, stops
at the steps, smells
the dryness of fall in
the late September air.

Remembers something
as the breeze tousles
his hair and forgets
for a moment the key
in his hand.

Something a young girl
said, maybe, or a
woman standing, breaking
a sprig of lilac,
turning: eyes damp.

Who can know what
stops him, what holds
the key suspended in
his hand, his head
turned as if to listen.

As he would not say,
locked on that moment,
his face expressionless
to tell joy or grief,
tempered, far away.

WOMAN IN A SWING

She dabs at her eyes,
sitting the porch swing,
and stares at the ridge
green-backed against
the sky.
                    She does not
know I see from my
shop door near her
garden, but I know
what has happened:

and who will fix the
faucet now when it
drips, drips long into
the night and replace
the burned-out light on

the cellar stairs? Who
will tramp with wet and
muddy feet and throw
carrots on the table?
Who will fix the lock?

Taken care of all her
life as if she were
a summer queen, her
audience is gone, the
forsaken garden dumb.

For this she weeps in
silence there and stares
at hills as young as
days when she still was
young, when
          she loved a
man, when she would have
broken the rocky
field and slept on straw
had he but let her.

GRANDFATHER GHOST

Out of summer heat
he comes with the odor
of broken earth woven
into his shirt,

sweat darkened front,
pants slack, shoes dark,
the back of his hands
crumbed with dirt.

Comes out of the dance of
summer heat to stand
in the barn's shadow,
browed eyes direct.

What have you come to tell
this time, old man, with
rough speech, cold advice,
gone kindness? Again

to say everything by
speaking of carrots, ways
to cure hay, the right
time of moon to cut hogs?

Old ghost, for God's
sake, old man, say what I
was to you, you in me, what
difference did we make?

Out of the shadow, he
returns to the dance of
summer heat, his shirt
still dark, his step

straight away from ways to
follow, toward lands where
praise is a dusty word
for which there is no call.

JACK WILSON'S INJURY

It was not the pain at all,
the first few mornings refusing
the excuses others made for him
to prop the leg and stay off it.

He shaved daily then, resting his
foot on the banister, watching
neighbors disappear into the fall
days, easy jokes with hometown bite.

When snow came, he sat at windows,
shirt untucked, crutches put away,
watching, bone nearly healed, storm clouds
wither, emptied of their fury.

And sat there still after spring rains
lost their look of daring and summer
brought the oddness of the sudden
strangers passing a forbidden house

which, like him, weathered without pain
into years. And only he, used
then to judgment, could understand
the power of its helplessness.

LE BREUN TALKS TO HIMSELF

Pull up a chair and sit
is not a placard on
my door, too much old man
for the pleasant enterprise,

not that there's no money
in it otherwise, quite
the other way around
in fact; maybe that's where

we get at the heart of
no nonsense: we've never
met, but I'm willing to bet
you have ways to suggest

turning my turnings into
profit not all for myself;
even more: pleasure for
those who don't know they

want pleasure yet. Forget
the plans you have for a new
house, your health, the weather
not quite itself this year.

I've lost my train of thought:
politics, God? Why, were you
in, I'd be out, supply met
quite aptly for yourself.

UNCLE ARTHUR

Well old uncle, old friend,
you have finally given
up the mind completely,
though you let it slip fast
these past two years, and have
taken the last of our
great family off, up
a final drive to the ridge.

The last time I wrote
about you was 1975
when you still took a drink
of whiskey and drove your
Plymouth down all roads,
getting lost for its
own sake, then using
directions for visits.

Farther back you made
moonshine in oak kegs, sold
it at dances where you
worked the music yourself,
playing your fiddle from
the shoulder rather than
the chin and dancing once
or twice with the ladies.

The question here is how
do I make you count

when you do not count,
as I do not count,
as even Socrates,
St. Augustine, Lincoln do
not count, only earth
separated from their names.

The last time I saw you,
you held a kitten you
had saved; you didn't know
my name. Today, rain pelts
the hayfield and the barn.
Were you back, you might tell
us what to say at this
end to an ancestral line.

2 What the Board Does

NATURAL

Cold days have come without
your losing your leaves this
fall, big trucks and big saws
taking the dull gold from

the postcard that you made,
leaving a landscape more
clearly seen, opposing
fields starker with the loss.

No doubt fall was your
season, too old for spring
dress, when green came dancing,
making you look your age.

Like most of us you died
in pieces, one year a new
scar that was next year gone,
a diversion for birds.

Of course we miss you, yet
know you aged to go
and so blame no one, the way
in fall, back from a trip

based on a photograph—
Ireland, maybe, or Key West—
we know the shot was
not undone by hungry waves

or changed streets, just as
you seemed to sense
the wonder gone in
you the way it would in us.

WHAT THE BOARD DOES

The board has nothing to say
to anyone other than
the worker after it
is taken from the tree.

It is in a different
country, and its relatives
have been left behind
to blend with their surroundings.

Of course groomed and handsome
it will make a cradle,
a table, for the normal
family, but being

completely happy is
something it cannot learn,
trying its best to please
by pleasing something else,

yet knowing, could it go
back, what changes to make,
goals set, below those familiar
clouds forever out of reach.

A PIECE OF CHERRY

Every nail and screw
in the shop
has its eye on me:

saws growl affection
while routers
make smooth promises,

drills pine
and sanders attend
on their cords;

all say they'll
make me art
I am so fine.

The square and level
talk patiently
in a corner,

their tones deep
and scribed
in some old language

I strain to hear.

WALNUT

Not as deep as bloodwood
nor as strong as oak,
feminine to us, neutral to
touch and delightfully shy
with its look of royalty,

we lean and linger over
subtle hues that change
from whiskey brown
to rose or purple,
then rub to luster

with delicate touch
the grain's direction that
may be long or circular
or curve back upon itself
to a lengthening center.

Widely imitated in
furniture marts for anyone
not particular, it's
without envy, lineal in
emotion, hard in thought

and in lumber yards holds
its corner, aloof until
chosen, becoming then
the mistress of our shop,
making the weakest of us

tremble at the cost, warning
against imitation or waste,
choosing only masters
who trade skill for consent,
perfect union without deceit.

RISING EARLY AGAIN

When I walk into the shop
I know something has changed.
Is it the pump again? Nope,
someone inside must have flushed
a toilet. Primed, it comes on.

My grandparents had an omen
once when a clock, stopped in
a drawer, began to alarm.
Later they learned that at the same
time one of their sisters died.

I've forgotten now the sister's name
or which one and forgotten,
too, the year it happened or when
they told me the story or the date
either one of them died.

I check pulleys, the saw blade for
fractures, a sack of fittings
in the corner where a blacksnake
surprised me once, even the lock
I know hasn't worked for years.

None of these things. Up early again
I sense, by the clouds, a slip in
the weather. There will be no sun
and it already Wednesday. Sleeping
in never feels right when you can.

WORKSHOP

We must freshen up the language
the young poet said, so we all
came together putting our hands
one on top of another as
if we were choosing sides for
a softball game and shook and shook
the walnut tree until nuts fell
on our heads like grocery limes.

And then he said, When reading poems
aloud don't make introductions
such chunks of candy they sour
the orange, and Dot Chevrolet said
that if a poem was not sweeter
than a chunk of chocolate or as
sleek as a Jaguar next to
a snow plow why risk breath at all.

Some of us went to the parking
lot, guilty with our tongues held,
and chased words up trees like dogs,
all in trouble we knew and Dot
cut a square off Sam's plug
of Brown's Mule but finding
she couldn't spit, threw her cud like
a simile against the muse.

Finding a metaphor was hard
because all the exceptions were

Ruths or Michelangelos,
but who taught trees to give nuts
Dot wanted to know while parents
of the drunk on the corner
gave him a house against the sky
and that other wall, Harvard.

PLUMB LEVEL AND SQUARE

I spent weeks spread out over
several months of an hour
or two a day trying
to get the chop saw square.

I never did. My trouble
was that I was using
a cheap combination Stanley
which hearsay said was good.

Just like pocket watches
I found that there isn't
one in a hundred that's
accurate, so experience

should have told me that trusting
a class in writing to
level my metaphors was
little short of plumb folly.

Miller's work, to me, was
plain beautiful, and Jane's
lines had the lean grace of
a race horse finishing.

So I tossed myself out
somewhere into the quarter
to spare them, not knowing
where I or this was going.

Turns out, it's in the square:
you lay your hands on a good
one, there's nothing known that
can't be true, at least for

a moment, the way the right
light can make a castle
out of a building that
by night is boards and nails.

GETTING THE DOWEL ROUND

There is nothing academic
about it; that you made
a D in algebra
doesn't matter when you need

to plane down another
thirty-seconds or cut sides
of a cradle on an angle
of seventeen degrees.

Boards warp, split and,
sometimes, run true, but they
do not speak good English,
nor do you when nothing's
left but to stop and start over.

Getting the dowel round, you
steal wit from usual learning,
just as the unguyed tree
chooses its own heavens.

The F you should have made
lies undetected; somehow,
through hands and movement, tools
and mind, the math is clear.

GLUING

I don't know exactly
how long it takes a joint
to bond, the directions
on the back of the bottle
about humidity
and temperature thrown
out the door on a cold
morning or hot afternoon.

It holds or it doesn't:
the stress on the rockers
of chairs in the corner might
outlast for years the slight
pressure on headboards.

My grandparents on both sides
stuck together, though one set
was forty years needing
mending, their furniture
made from lumber drawn by
thick-legged horses, sawn
and dried, but I don't think
glue was stronger back then.

You design the fit well,
with no promise, and take
your chances, hoping for
magic that comes only
after long hours: the piece
more than wood, glue more than
a squirt from a bottle.

DUST

Imagine a closed-up house,
sheets a menagerie,
windows changing their shadows
on hardwood floors as hours
sift days, weeks powder months.

Here in one afternoon
the saw has cast my footprints
to the door and back again,
to the bench where, lifted,
the square has left its edge.

Clean it today, it's back
again tomorrow, eager
as ever to say, Yes, yes,
you kissed me from your mind,
but that was yesterday.

In fast-forward time I
brush the boards I have sawn,
then brush after I sand,
the air a storm that hangs
and jostles and remains.

The house was anyone's,
but now it's mine, tenants
that I knew since childhood
moved, dust that can't be cleaned,
yet lingering, informing

and joining the storm that
begins to settle to
slow-motion again, its
origin the housekeeper's bane
and still a mystery.

FOSSIL IN CEMENT

There is a fossil of
a pine needle near the screen
door and for a moment,
the sun not yet up,
I bend down and study
it with my fingernail.

The man who poured this floor
or had it poured was a young
man who letting it dry
overnight did not note
the wind that blew it here,
so intent upon his roof.

One day he had a shop;
the next, his job took him
to other towns and so
I live that dream he may
or may not have forgotten,
but old now either way.

A different dream, not
so romantic after all,
except from a distance where
the saw blade meeting board
or a hammer bending steel
reminds us of something lost.

It's like a wing, or more like
a V of wings as cries
head south, the tip the head
of its leader, or perhaps
a windblown seed, down long
before the bouncing cone.

GRINDSTONE

The sun is out today,
bringing with its false hope
cold weather; on beaches
somewhere nearly naked
girls are turning themselves,
perhaps under umbrellas.

I'm not glad to be here
but not unglad not to
be there either, working
inside at something not
burdened with particulars
that I'll miter later.

Against the wall below
a window is a grindstone
once worked by my grandfather,
over which I have built
a small table; you can
see the handle I turned

for him hot summer days,
splash of rusty water,
wooden, right angled like
a bicycle pedal,
stuff on top of stuff with
stuff balanced above it.

They are putting lotion
on themselves on those beaches,
round and round in the sun.
Don't you ever tire of work?
I do not say, his hair
full, gray above the blade.

MUSIC BOX

When a part of the whole
is scrutinized, after
the sanding and sanding,
just before the stain is
applied, it is imperfect still,

just as the job the frost
has done on the hillside
with its one untouched tree
seems faulty, as if frost
might not be diligent.

We don't want to leave it so,
knowing there are those,
perhaps with less skill
but better eye, whose one
talent in life is judgment.

Take this inlay I've worried
hours and hours; set aside,
then picked up and held to
light, there is the seam
that stain won't cover.

But other boards, pretending
to be unflawed, which you
know are not, are ready
and demand the movement,
Autumn Leaves, perhaps, as
you chill and let it go.

SMELL

Sometimes the smell of yesterday's
sawdust in the shop
is enough to make the day start
slowly, remembering

a barn loft half-filled with hay my
grandparents traded
for town while my back was turned
away at college,

or the cleaning rod whittled from basswood
that the store porch
loafer made for my first shotgun
when I was twelve.

Yet, mostly, days start forward now,
just after dew
has lost its favor, sun scything
toward the south,

when sense balks, to say, Yes, but where's
that farm now, its
fields grown to trees both wide and tall
for lumber?

or, The last shotgun you fired was
at a rattlesnake
that you missed by a foot in your
neighbor's yard.

All right, I usually say, throwing
open the door,
you're not my father, brushing hay from
my neck, dumping

shells from my pockets, wondering
if smell is only
a trick from the past, fooling us with what
we thought we'd be.

THE BOX

The box dresses itself
in red and green
wrapping, though
it is not Christmas.

Sometimes it sits
on glass tables
where fine legs
cross and uncross;

sometimes it climbs
to the top shelf
and watches handsomely
from a child's closet.

Critics who grow
impatient try to
assign it a hand
to reveal itself

or make of its
beauty the hollowness
behind the blue eye
of a doll.

But it is a box,
it does not say,
as simple as spots
on a fawn

or a morning
where light alone
wakes
the sleeping bird.

SNAKE

Where the yard ends in brush
just before the woods, birds
not of a feather have
gathered in the pear tree.

Though most have found a throat
it is the jay who has
become spokesman of
the group, preacher of sorts,

shrieking about beak, breast,
down and retribution.
The choir around joins in
with every inch of hate

the tree can balance while
one thumb-size mourner cries,
All my pretty ones, oh
hell's kite, did you say all?

When in a moment the
alarm is over, birds
returned to their private songs,
there is a shiver maybe

only God can see, the tree
again settled to its
old ease, through the seasons
tempered by such banter.

CHEST OF DRAWERS

The colder it gets, the more
trees get undressed, standing
nearly naked here on this
coldest day of the year,

while I turn their fallen
neighbors into drawers
we will use next summer
to store winter clothes.

We who see them beautiful
dead as alive, their blond
straight lines, their secret grain
revealed by careful stain,

think always of diminution
when we hug them, live,
measuring with our arms
their circumference, cocking

our eye for the felling,
imagining their rich scent
as they are ricked in shelters
to cure fair and elegant.

Coldest day of the year.
Yet then, as now, when they
dance again in loveliness
and we shuck to little

or nothing, the certain fall:
we were bred so, the ripe
nut husked by the squirrel,
the fare so pleasing to the hand.

SUN ON THE SAW TABLE

Sun comes through the end-vent
on the east side of the building
just under the roof and hits
the table saw blade squarely.

For a moment I feel that I'm
in a pyramid in Egypt
on just the right day when
something magical happens:

a stream triggered by some
sensored lock begins to flow,
a vault opens, or a skirted
scribe flees from his calculations.

I don't know if it happens
only once a year; it is not
the winter solstice and already
I'm on my return to Georgia

whcre I open the door and turn
back to see the beam is gone.
I wish I knew how to make
the moment linger, magic stick,

capture from darkness some new
theory that prolongs wonder.
How they must have felt too, those
ancients, busy with wraps and ointments,

that work would outlive invention,
the light through a chink above
them a momentary distraction
from their safekeeping of tombs.

CUT ONCE

When something is broken,
the way a belt snaps on
a motor or a board
is cut an inch too short,

your first response is to
stare or cry out or curse
and then with useless hands
try how it used to fit

as if with hope you can
undo that moment and in
the one before stop what
was done because you thought.

Once, in wartime or when
replacement parts were fifty
dollars beyond a new
work shirt, some used resource:

string was cheap or the welder
down the road a good man
with a torch had you patience
to wait your turn for him.

But no one can fix a board
too short, just as someone
after a stroke is no
longer Uncle Billy

or Aunt Ruth, gray head on
a pillow, a walker up
steps, the board meant for
their porch swing something else.

TOMORROW, A SOFA TABLE

Every completed piece
has its signature, just
as the time to make it
depends on light and heart
and materials on hand.

The book case with glass doors
is an old man who has
time to read *Don Quixote*,
the quilt rack a young girl
who is planning her wedding.

The gate made from slats from
a family barn is
a man who collects guns
and diaries, but did
not know his grandfather,

jewelry box a woman
who saw herself ugly
as a child, but now loves
New Orleans—good sense
in dress and choosing lovers.

What stamp we use, what
wood we choose to stain,
varnish, or let weather,
we learned from stickball on
our street, weeds in the pasture.

Each piece its own story,
rolling up our sleeves, pants'
legs loose around the ankles,
moving lumber around
until we get bitten.

ROCKING HORSE

It is what others do not know
and you do not say about
the rocking horse that make it plain
to you, heirloom to them:

the maple board you traded to
a Kentucky friend for
a piece of walnut for the saddle,
the router bit you bought

for the nostrils that you've never
used again, back and forth
trips to tack rooms and, finally,
to a cobbler for the reins.

It would be pretended interest
should you try to explain
the day spent shaping handles,
doweling the curved mane,

ears stopped, eyes averted to see
their child bent in gallop,
touching their fingers across legs
and tail, saying, Like velvet.

It is what you do not say and they
do not know about horses
and Lawrence that speeds sanding
and lightens afternoons,

the plainness of wood and mistakes
and returning, the grace of
eyes and mouth become effortless
in the face of praise.

3 Quick Edges

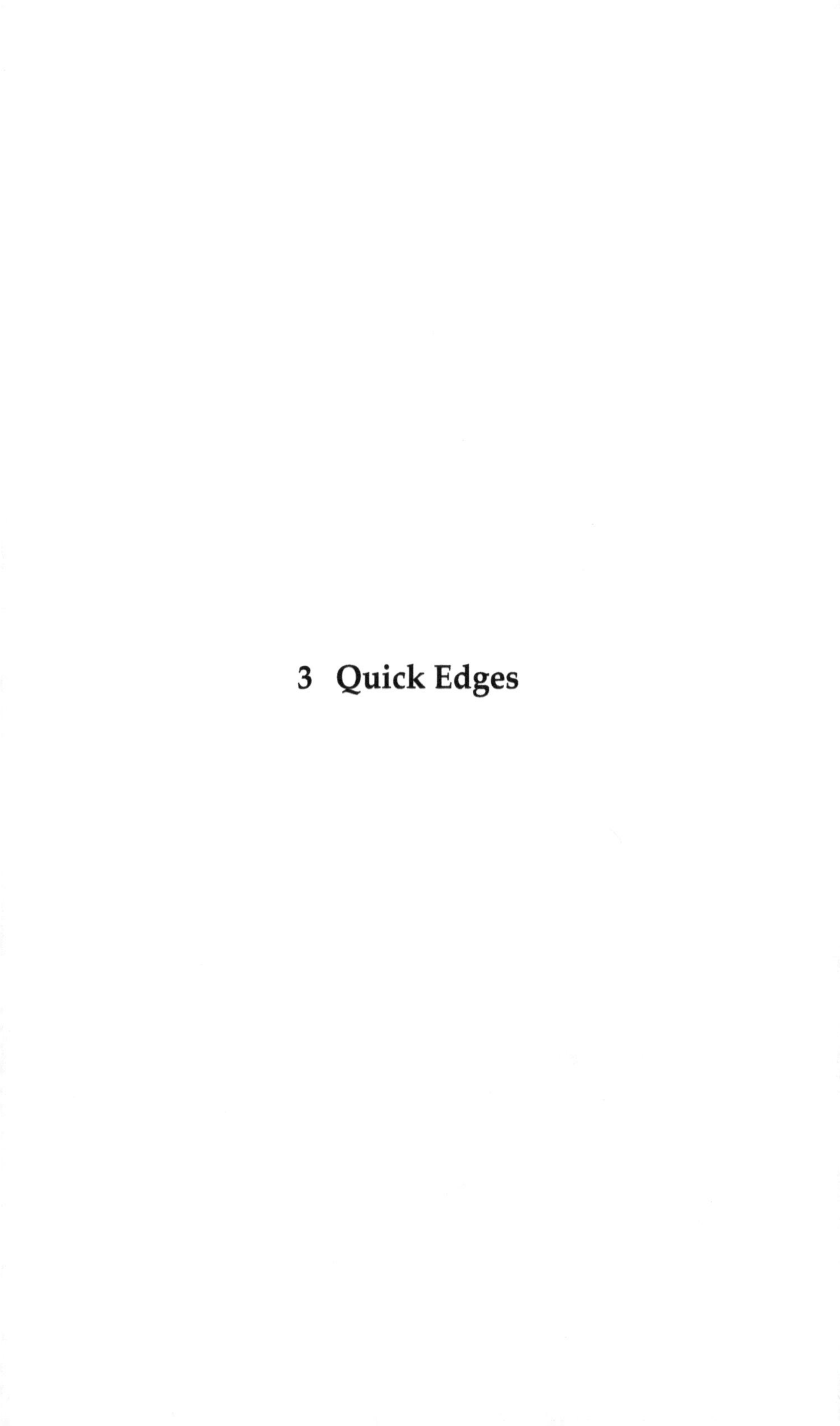

VISITOR

Looking up from my rule where
I've just measured two feet,
six and seven-eighths inches,
I see a snake come through
the hole where the screen door
has warped away from the jamb.

Tasting, smelling, whatever
snakes do, it esses itself,
a hundred times slower
than it takes to tell, out
the front door to disappear
in St. Augustine grass.

I measure again and set
the fence, yet, counting the time
I need to recover,
I know I'll be measuring
again. What the hell was
it doing, tree snake, rat
snake, garter snake, racer?

I was right the first time.
I use a stop block and cut
the rails. Then, hopeless trader,
I turn to brush off dust
at the door; half an hour, three
eggs in its belly, likely.

NO ANTIQUES

When she walked in, all I
could say was whoa. The way
she touched her finger on
the saw, looked up and then
away, so fast you'd swear
she hadn't seen the dust.

Her man was a round face
in boots you knew somewhere
belonged to a red pickup
always washed, not now or
ever with a dog in back.

They'd heard I sold antiques,
baby cradles from long back
in the hills my relatives
made, hand-painted plates,
maple rocking chairs, quilts.

Fumbling till past noon,
I built everything like
a chair with one leg short;
I didn't ask their names,
surprised they found my shop.

Then finally gave up, not
guessing, growing up, I'd
never outgrow shyness,

the need to pose and act
but some way tell my heart.

Whoever they are somewhere
down the road with their misgivings,
I give them thoughts: Who was
that odd man anyway;
how *does* he make a living?

SPLINTER IN THE HAND

The difference between a field
and meadow is that a field has
too many ironweeds to be one

as the difference between youth
and old age is that a pimpled
face has turned into two big ears
in a robe, muttering, Who, What?

If you see the connection you
are either from a farm, old, crazy
or know two words are sometimes three.

The things that don't seem to make sense
but do or the things that seem to make
perfect sense and do are the same.

They do not have to be pretty
to be beautiful and they can
do it with or without nature,
youth, old age or fixed syllables.

Take a splinter in the hand: now
what gladness is there in that pain?
just, perhaps, plenty when it's gone.

EPITHALAMIUM

The quilt rack I'm building
for my nephew was commissioned
in a silent deal: I'll make
you one on the promise
I'm spared the ceremony.

He made no promise, nor
was asked for one outside
the conversation I
tied the ribbon on of
present without presence.

How could he? Those other
ones who see the moment
of their lives beyond the whims
of sickness, golf, or I'd
rather be in Georgia.

It's three-quarters finished,
the arches a ring of
laminated oak,
dowels, stretchers, and base
a half year in the planning

to remind them on their June
day of Christmases
and the hard snowy nights
shared by their ancestors
in new, west Virginia.

In my mind, except for
flowers, I've played their song,
done the dance and built my
part of the bargain. Where they'll
get the quilt I don't know.

SHOP WINDOW

Most things here are violent:
the planer, the router,
all the heavy saws that long
for misdirection to chew
wood down to the bone.

When my brother was small
and I was little taller,
the doctor rode his Ford
up to the back door, stepped
off onto the porch and spat
his way into the kitchen.

He moved through the house
like a sawmill until
he reached the bedroom of
our mother, sick, we thought
dying, and pressed to her hand
a vial from his pocket.

After the noise, the fume,
the disarray pieced together,
after the uncertainty
of birdsong is renewed,
the measure of ointment
administered, we are

spared a moment only
by the crafted desk, its oak

finish, safety from blade
and fever, as if assured
forever summer lightning,
our shrubbery dressed in snow.

CARDINAL

Where I left the screen open
to carry in a sheet of
plywood, a female cardinal
has flown inside the door,

taking on a bar clamp
and a rafter before,
what someone first surely
meant, knocking herself silly

against the window glass.
A brown feather and herself,
not in that order, huddled
on the concrete floor.

In my hand she is all
feathers, not part of her
summer nest in gardenias
or her fellows, eyeing

the plump seeds of autumn.
When we both regain our
senses, she pecks my thumb
once to let us know,

then rises up at the door
to the first tree she finds,
where, on cue, she flies and I
step back to a careful life.

THE HOUND AT THE GATE

The hound that will not hunt
is at the gate again
this morning, tail flagging,
head down, whimpering.

It has been this way each
morning for a week, even
though at dawn today, as I
was looking past the door

of the shop, he was not
there. At first I thought
I had made a mistake.
But no: there was the whistle
of a hawk, a bowl of blue,

and suddenly ideas for both
a wine rack and votive lights;
anyone with a steady mind
would have known that a day

beginning with two plans
was doomed. And sure enough,
at eight o'clock there he
was again, his belly empty

as the road that now is dust.
By afternoon, of course,
when I have no patience
left, he will go trembling

off to some neighbor's house.
You see the kind of dog he
is: he never barks, has
not a rabbit in his head,

half on his back, nor glancing
up, he dreams the Master
Carpenter, that would not bite
one tick for his return.

EDGES OF ROADS

Of all country things, I suppose
I know best the edges of roads,
not berms where grass grows down to sides
of ditches, like on interstates,

or even where animals feed
at dusk, where cans congregate with
wrappers and the small dead are bounced
off below the cruising vultures.

I mean the trails behind the line
of woods and brush several yards off
where whatever watches can see
all that passes, not seen itself.

Hunters will know the place I mean
where on wet fall days they can move
silently, far enough from home,
but not in so deep they can get lost.

Lovers know it best, slipping off
on weekday afternoons or weekend
nights, pushing back convertible
tops, reaching for fragments of sky.

Seeing and not being seen are what
I want to say, not in hiding
but in league with fringes, knowing
what roads don't know of things that stay,

the way a child, who isn't lost, kneels
out of sight, urging with a straw
a beetle along, while through the town
anxious voices cry out his name.

SHOP VAC

Short belly on wheels,
beads for a neck,
it's as if it not only
has a mind of its own
but chooses to be opponent.

To visitors it is
a model citizen,
well-behaved
as a child asleep,
obedient as a wall,

but when awake, come time
to clean, it's a weasel
on a wire, running
from or chasing every
occupant in the shop.

Tangled up or simply
caught, it tolerates no
reprimand, reversing blame:
as if a machine could
unplug itself alone!

Somehow, it makes our words
about it facile, its voice
clear if raucous in tone,
making sure we know it
sees but does not fear the broom.

HOUSE ON MUNDAY ROAD

Where the road curves back
against the hill to miss
the creek there is a green house
in the adjacent bottom.

A man killed himself
there when I was a boy
but no adult would say why;
I do not know his name.

Now there are chickens in
the yard and a clothes line
with a pole holding sheets
a few inches off the ground.

How long ago must it
seem to my daughter and son
when they think after I
say, When I was a boy.

And how long ago it
seems to me imagining
the dying Keats thinking
of when he was a boy.

The man who killed himself
was about my age; I
cannot say what there is
about this house that offers

its green peace. Even if
they might wish to say, I
do not know if any know
why others choose to die.

SUMMER STORM

We have reached the time
of year of summer storms
and yesterday a small girl
down the road was struck
and killed by lightning.

The case was pictured
bold-faced in the paper
and we were shocked the more
by her large dog, seated
and panting beside her.

Drinking with two hands
I brace my morning
with black coffee and walk
from tools to window
assessing my own yard.

Later, having gathered
and piled the broken limbs
in order, all will send
the usual cards that
rhyme our quiet sympathy.

Of course, it is the time
of year for storms, but now
the neighborhood is
overwrought and moody:
the summer sky of last

night's lightning as white
as winter, and no one
to say for sure it was
but a summer birth,
with that sullen difference.

THE BREAK

There is pain
in the broken corner
of the walk
where a tire,

an iron box,
or simply ice
and weather
made its bite.

Cracked in grass
and apart,
it grows,
a crooked tooth.

Remote, that breaking;
impossible to say
what future
or original design.

An old man's ache
acquired painlessly,
like rheumatism,
in an old yard.

WORKPLACE

The day back is always hard
for those whose clothes are no
longer new even when they are:

a motor with a new cord
trying to adjust to different
wiring, brushing off rust;

the stack of forms that on
last watch was a laugh away
from computer office works.

Always there, as spring comes,
summer into autumn, tree
that changes never changing.

If we only know it is hard
for them when it is hard for us,
both become hands to a clock

we hate yet cannot do without,
we remain aloof, smiling
at their steel-eyed pleasantness,

listening to them interpret
the new manual as if they
had built it themselves or ripped
it apart a thousand times.

TURKEY-SHOOT CHAMPION

As if notice counts, your picture
in some journal nobody
reads or everybody reads:
the marbles played for and won.

It's part of the package, pretense,
jealousy, acting what
has been played better
to few who know the difference.

If not always, take the tired man
with the long gun on his cabin
porch, turkey-shoot champion,
now a book with brown pages.

Not better to have been the loser,
not worse, a leaf one day turned,
passage dropped, seeing
in the stream of words a white stone.

The necessary blank to round it out,
for the old, the stroke, for the young,
not all blind, the happy union
of luck and youth, the urgent hope.

THE DEATH OF THE WOOD RASP

The rasp with its rat's tail
driven deep into a length
of sawn-off rake handle,
which once courted only

walnut and mahogany
and angled its delicate teeth
along the nape of batons,
has lost its rage for action

since the fresh orbital
sander, making obsolete
all but the finest wet-dry
paper, arrived in its box.

The wire brush itself is
astonished, knowing that
once only the promise of
friction freed its hunger.

But like a stiff mink with
its teeth frozen open,
it lies alone on a shelf
under a layer of dust,

which long ago could not
have dreamed the new finish,
roughhewn handle, its love-
making grating of youth.

FLIPPING THE SWITCH

It is language with small
vocabulary between blades
and wood,

the way first lovers
say words soft and cruel,
as night speaks
to trees in summer;

snarling, biting at grain
contrary,
thriving on darkness,

the nature of speech
between old friends: blunt
and cautious.

RIGHT ANGLE BLADE

The mattock, which I originally
kept in the garage
and should have left there, has fallen
from its corner, asked me to dance.

What should I say, that it is no
substitute for
a backhoe, something clever only
to myself? It can't be fooled.

It knows that and digs ditch from way
back to my dad's saying,
Carry a hundred pound sack of feed
to the pickup if you want girls.

Oh, it has its more truth than secrets
worn in its handle
from digging someone's grave in tune
with bawdy humor to cover fear.

Step up, step up, it says, or, now down,
stay seated and let
the movement swirl you to hilltops
where crowds gather in small rain,

lest in useful moment you hide
with false tools in bold
color to forget the music that leaks
from the ground, that teaches to swing.

MUTINY

The gang has gathered around
this morning demanding
a meeting, but I say
I won't listen, not today.

I close the door and look
off toward mountains I
can't see, just imagine,
and think of all the shrugs

I have not made, the shrugs
that most of them should have
made, but didn't, withheld
that a day might happen.

What days we have missed that
days might happen we must
imagine, chests stored in
mountains that erode away.

At first there is silence,
then the low rumble of
motors starting, the whine
of blades, circle of knives.

I can't stop their motion;
as if alive they'll bring
fruition, though it costs their
bearings, the whirl of their lives.

"AND SO GOOD-BYE . . ."

Tennessee Williams, *The Glass Menagerie*

I lay the bastard file on a short
two-by-four nailed between the studs;
it rolls toward the edge until I
wedge it with a piece of molding.

It is raining and other tools
are quiet as if they are saying
goodbye to each other, the way
people after Christmas say goodbye.

We've finished another project,
all left to do now a final
brush of varnish, some light sanding,
one last flick of a fingernail.

If ending means new beginning,
we're idle enough here to want
to believe it without speeches,
an unease in our resolve.

But what crosses the room is not
what passes between the thoughts
of people, the warmth of ancestry,
the nod of head, arrest of eye.

Not a question of happiness
or unhappiness, we have
worked together as water works
together to make a stream,

as trees work together to make
a cove; only I can tell their
farewells, only I can say that
today we are going away.

www.ingramcontent.com/pod-product-compliance
Lightning Source LLC
Chambersburg PA
CBHW022203150726

47992CB00002B/925